APERTURE MASTERS OF PHOTOGRAPHY

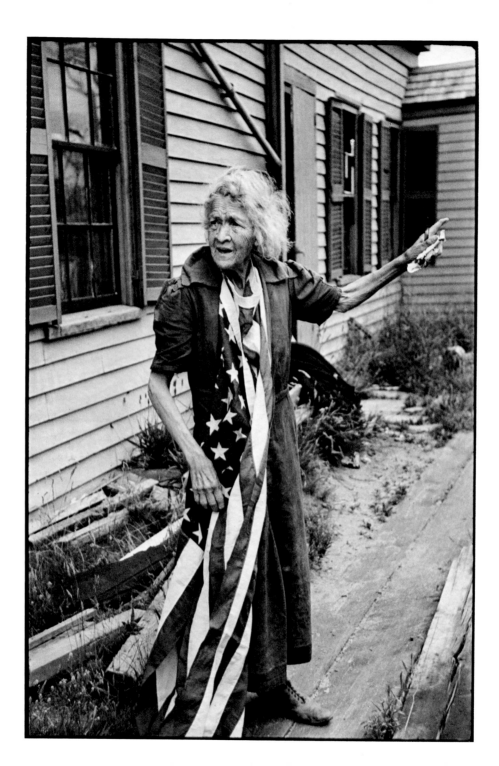

HENRI CARTIER-BRESSON

MASTERS OF PHOTOGRAPHY

APERTURE

Printed and bound in Hong Kong.
Library of Congress Catalog Number: 87-70205
ISBN: 0-89381-744-9

This 1997 edition is a coproduction of Könemann Verlags Gmbh
and Aperture Foundation, Inc.

Aperture Foundation publishes a periodical, books, and portfolios of fine photography to communicate with photographers and creative people everywhere. A complete catalog is available upon request. Address: 20 East 23rd Street, New York, New York 10010. Phone: (212) 598-4205. Fax: (212) 598-4015.

The Aperture Masters of Photography series is distributed in the following territories through Könemann Verlags Gmbh, Bonner Str. 126, D-50968 Köln. Phone: (0221) 93 70 39-0. Fax: (0221) 93 70 39-9: *Continental Europe, Israel, Australia, and the Pacific Rim.* The series is distributed in the following territories through Aperture: *Canada:* General Publishing, 30 Lesmill Road, Don Mills, Ontario, M3B 2T6. Fax: (416) 445-5991. *United Kingdom:* Robert Hale, Ltd., Clerkenwell House, 45-47 Clerkenwell Green, London EC1R OHT. Fax: 171-490-4958. *All other territories:* Aperture, 20 East 23rd Street, New York, New York 10010. Phone: (212) 505-5555. Fax: (212) 979-7759.

For international magazine subscription orders for the periodical *Aperture*, contact Aperture International Subscription Service, P.O. Box 14, Harold Hill, Romford, RM3 8EQ, England. Fax: 1-708-372-046. One year: £30.00. Price subject to change.

To subscribe to the periodical *Aperture* in the U.S.A. write Aperture, P.O. Box 3000, Denville, NJ 07834. Phone: 1-800-783-4903. One year $40.00.

K 2   K4   K6   K8   K7   K5   K3   K1

"Actually it's quite true that he's not waiting
for anyone since he's not made any appointment,
but the very fact that he's adopting this ultra-receptive posture
means that by this he wants to help chance along,
how should I say, to put himself in a state of grace with chance,
so that something might happen, so that some one might drop in."

—André Breton, *Entretiens* (*1913–1952*)
(*Idées/Gallimard, p. 150*)

Photography has not changed since its origin except in its technical aspects, which for me are not a major concern.

Photography appears to be an easy activity; in fact, it is a varied and ambiguous process in which the only common denominator among its practitioners is their instrument. What emerges from this recording machine does not escape the economic constraints of a world of waste, of tensions that become increasingly intense and of insane ecological consequences.

"Manufactured" or staged photography does not concern me. And if I make a judgment, it can only be on a psychological or sociological level. There are those who take photographs arranged beforehand and those who go out to discover the image and seize it. For me, the camera is a sketch book, an instrument of intuition and spontaneity, the master of the instant which—in visual terms—questions and decides simultaneously. In order to "give a meaning" to the world, one has to feel oneself involved in what he frames through the viewfinder. This attitude requires concentration, a discipline of mind, sensitivity, and a sense of geometry. It is by great economy of means that one arrives at simplicity of expression. One must always take photos with the greatest respect for the subject and for oneself.

To take photographs is to hold one's breath when all faculties converge in the face of fleeing reality. It is at that moment that mastering an image becomes a great physical and intellectual joy.

To take photographs means to recognize—simultaneously and within a fraction of a second—both the fact itself and the rigorous organization of visually perceived forms that give it meaning. It is putting one's head, one's eye and one's heart on the same axis.

As far as I am concerned, taking photographs is a means of understanding which cannot be separated from other means of visual expression. It is a way of shouting, of freeing oneself, not of proving or asserting one's own originality. It is a way of life.

Henri Cartier-Bresson

Córdoba, Spain, 1933

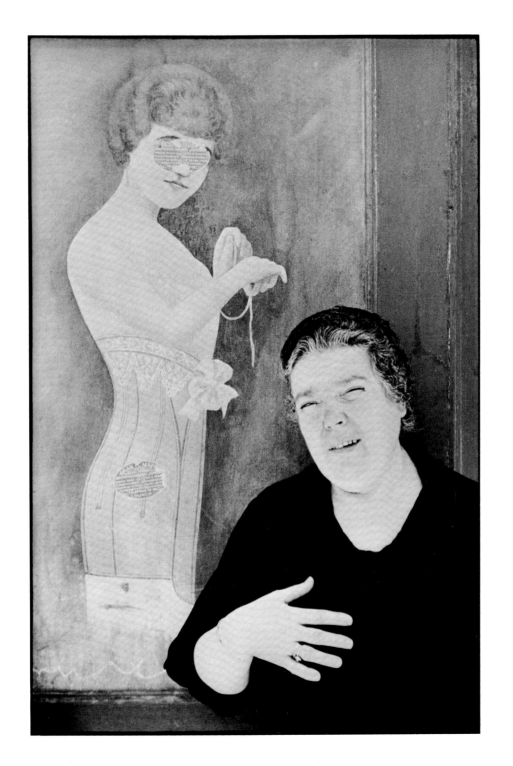

Taxi drivers, Berlin, 1932

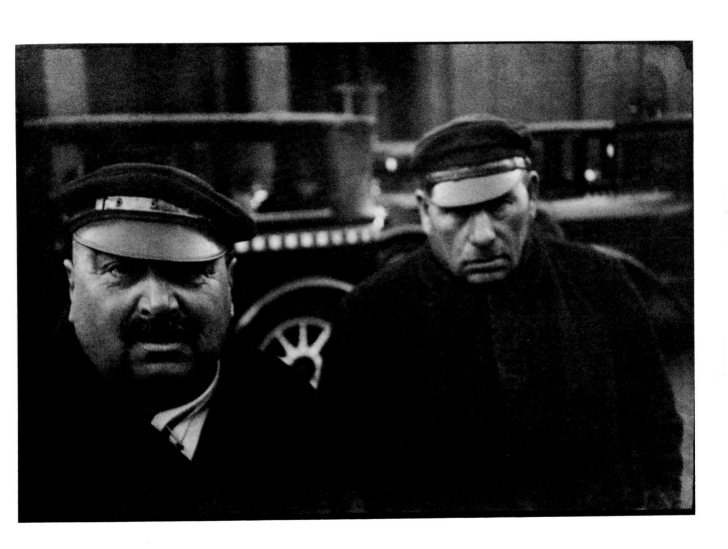

Marseilles, 1932

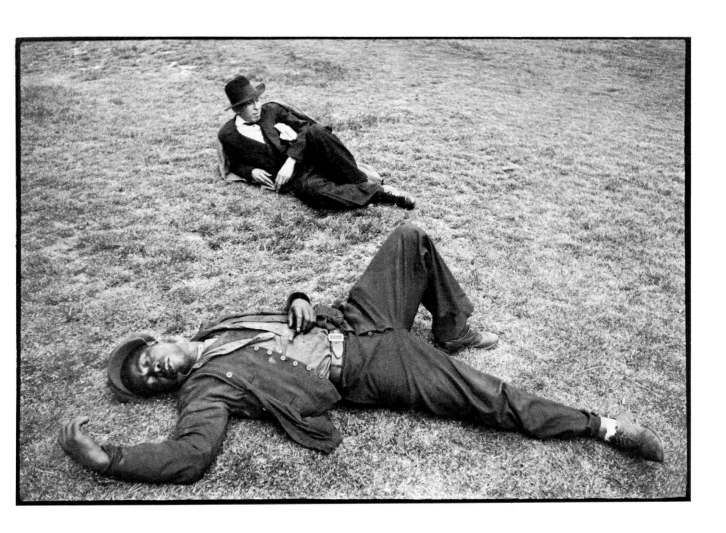

Brussels, 1932

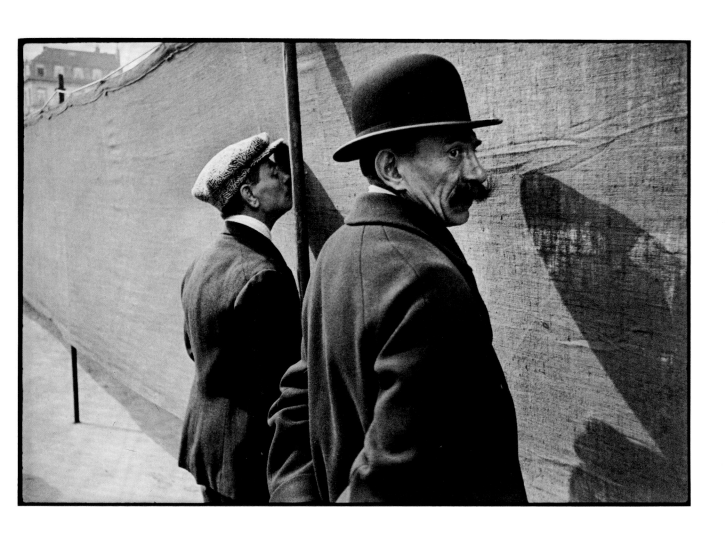

Seville, Spain, 1933

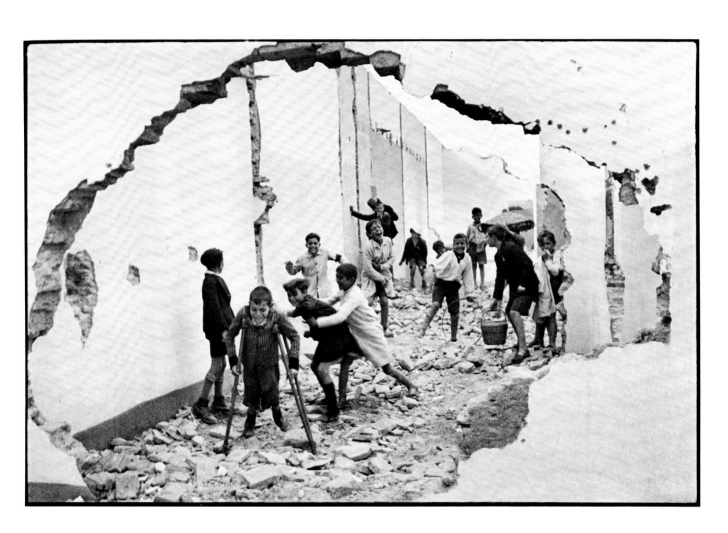

Seville, Spain, 1932

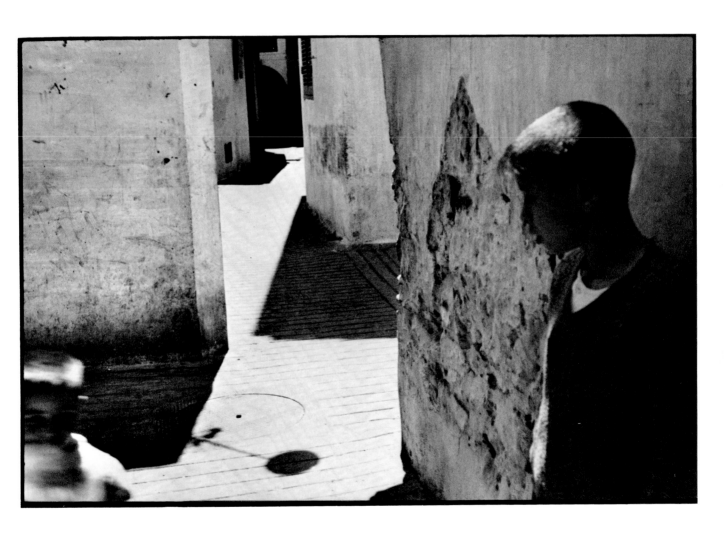

Alicante, Spain, 1932

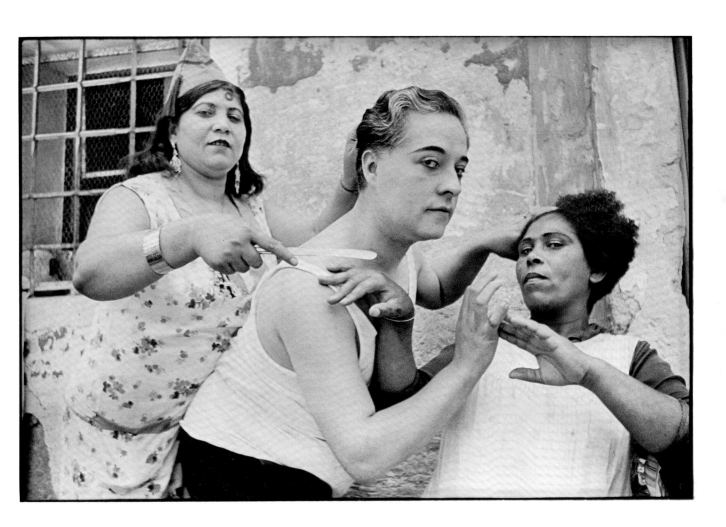

Madrid, 1933

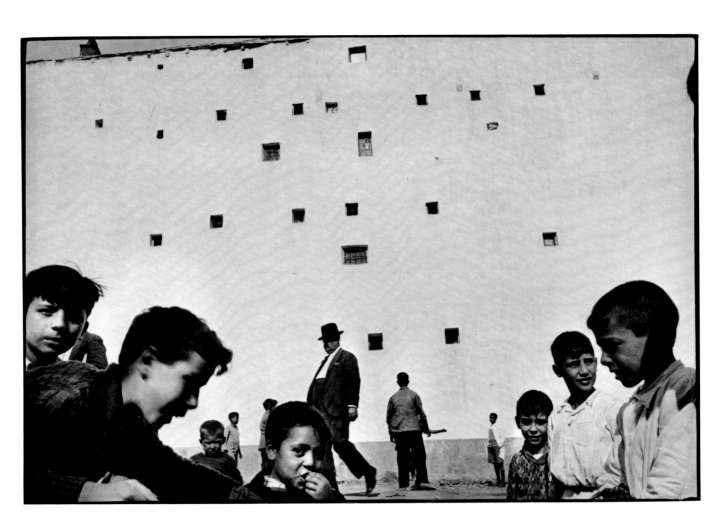

Arena at Valencia, Spain, 1933

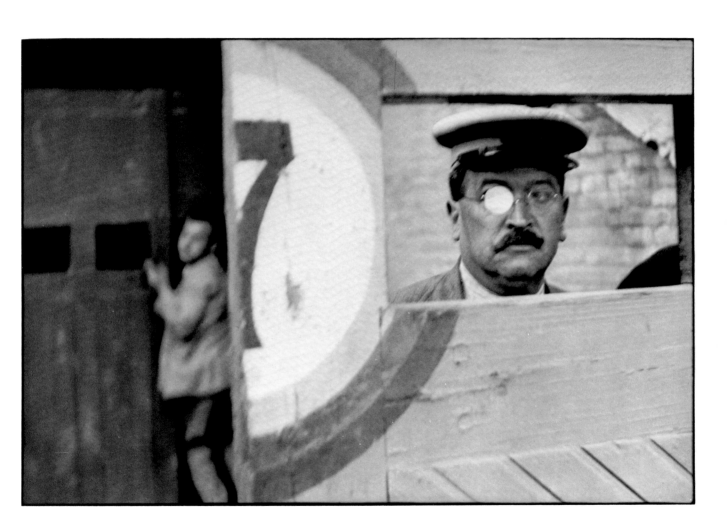

By the Marne River, 1938

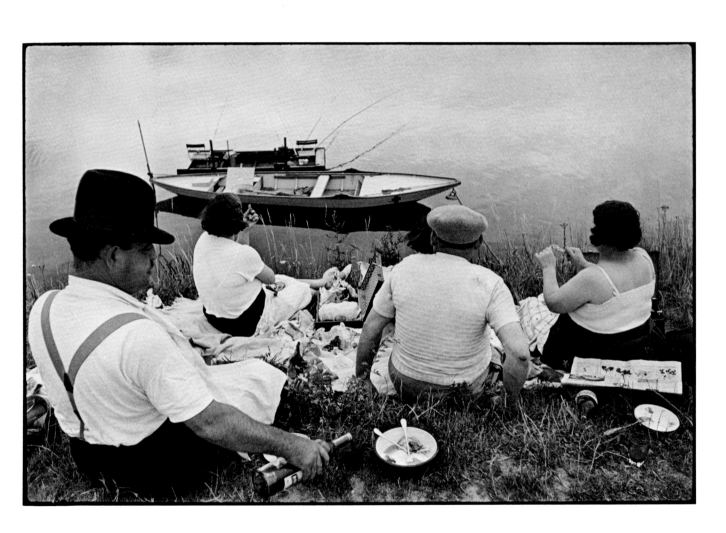

Barrio Chino, Barcelona, Spain, 1933

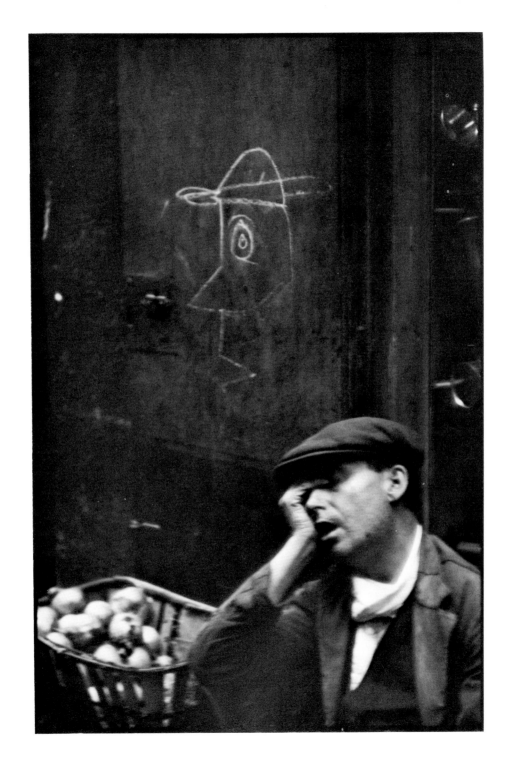

Quai Saint-Bernard, Paris, 1932

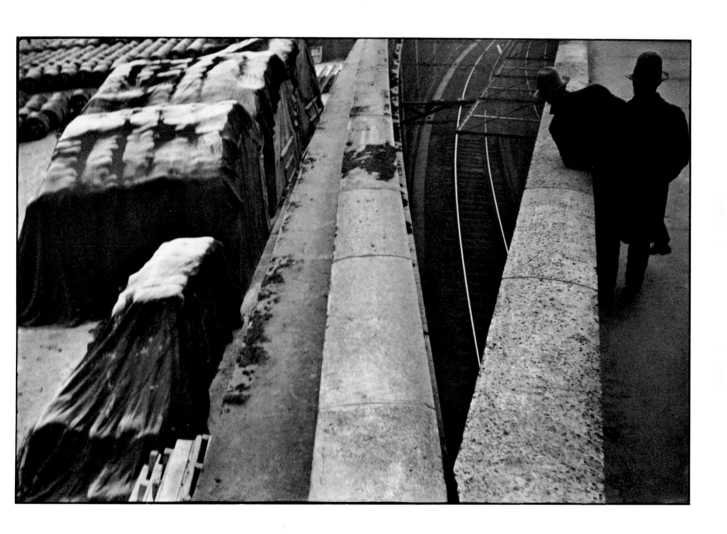

Mexico, 1934

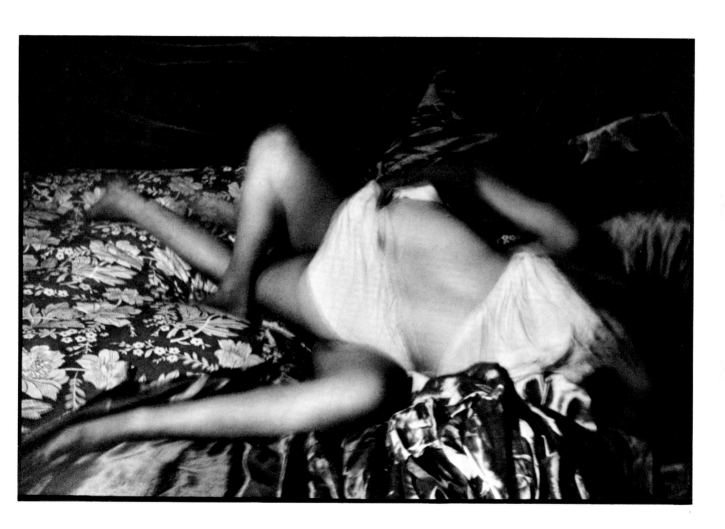

33

Quai de Javel, Paris, 1932

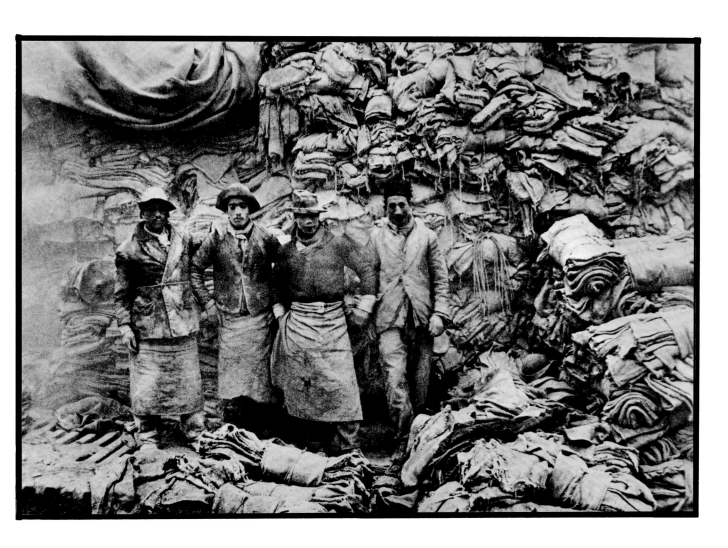

Valencia, Spain, 1933

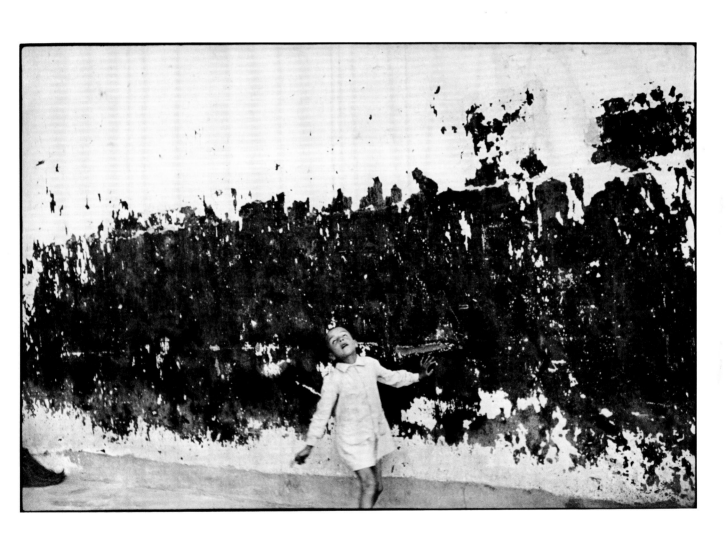

Behind the Saint-Lazare station, Paris, 1932

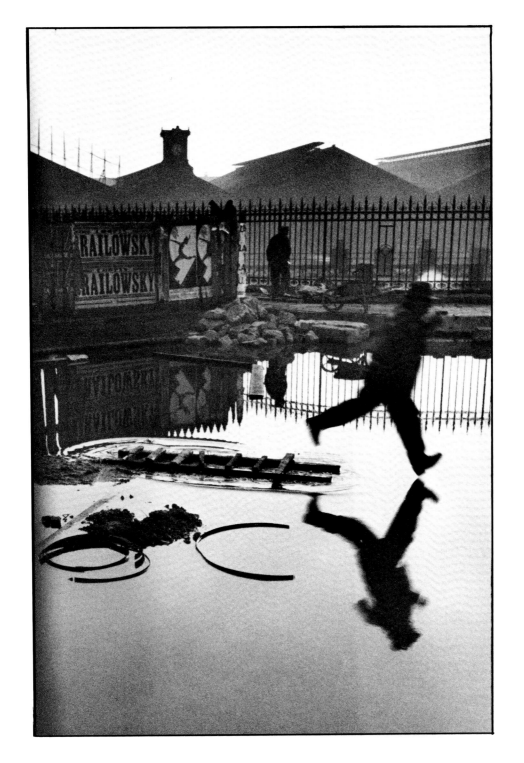

Trieste, Italy, 1933

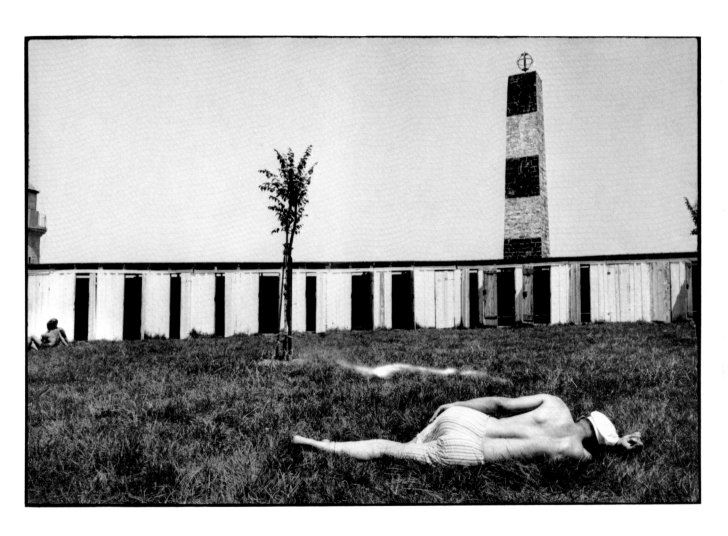

Irène and Frédéric Joliot-Curie, Paris, 1945

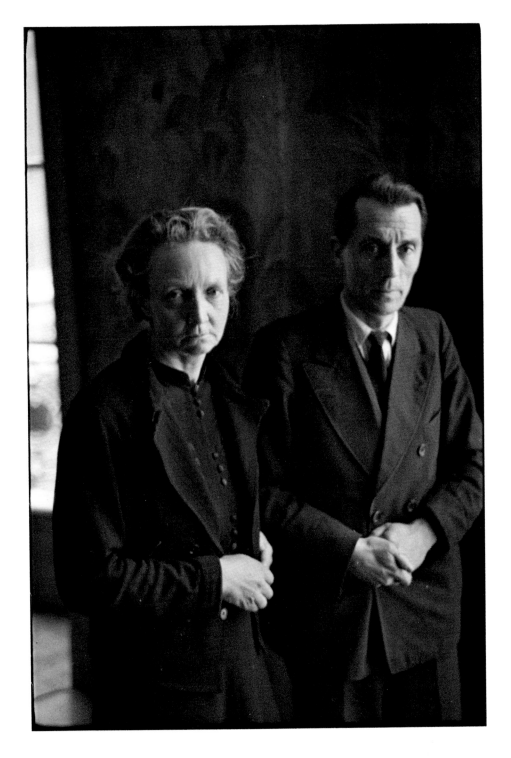

Cardinal Pacelli at Montmartre, Paris, 1938

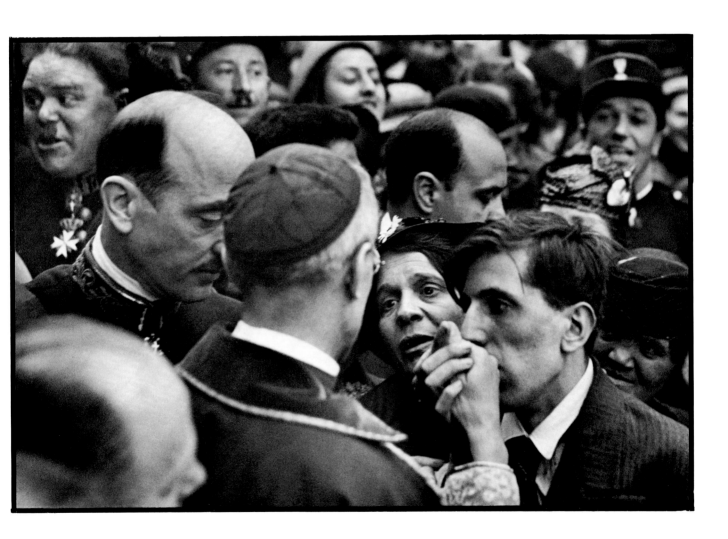

In a deportee camp, a Gestapo informer is recognized by a
woman she has denounced: Dessau, Germany, 1945

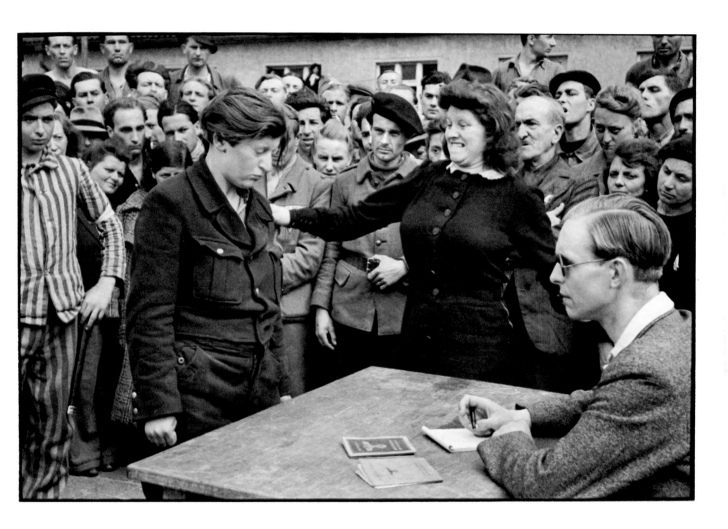

The Berlin Wall, 1963

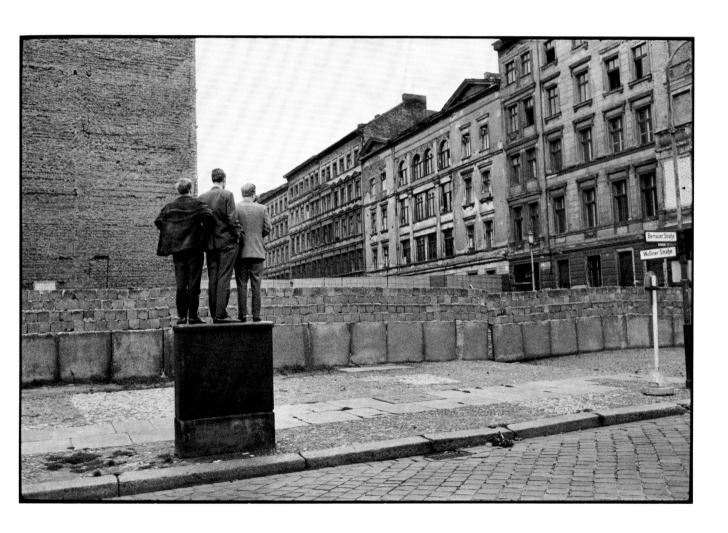

Hyde Park, London, 1938

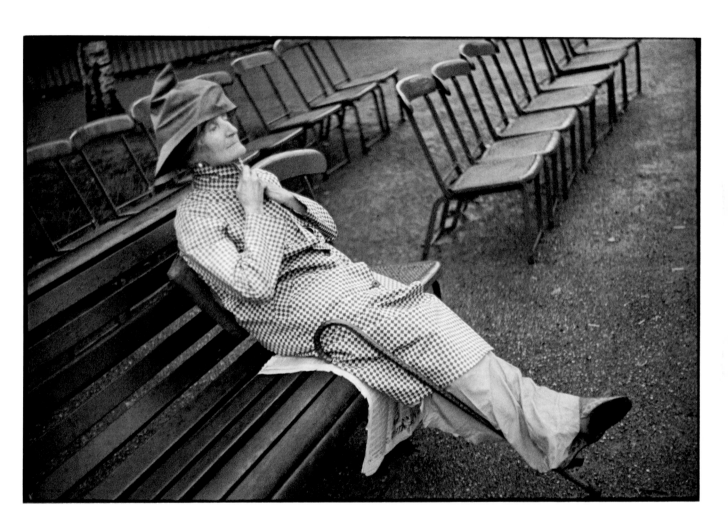

Trafalgar Square on the day George VI was crowned: London, 1938

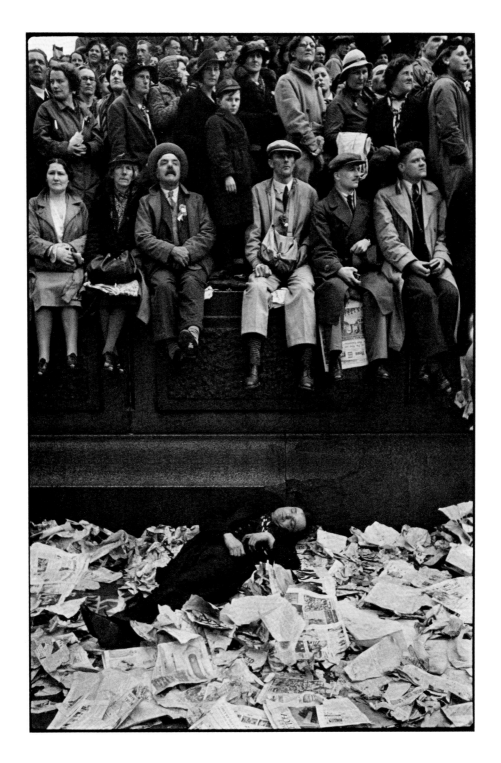

At the Curragh race course near Dublin, 1955

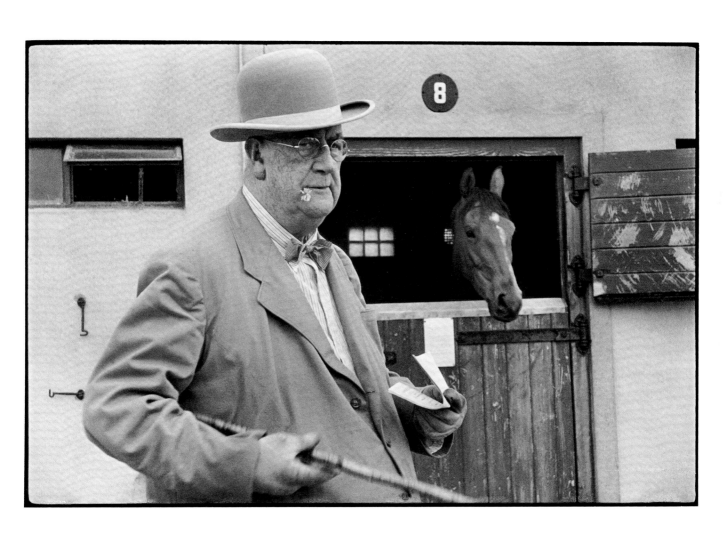

Henri Matisse, Venice, 1944

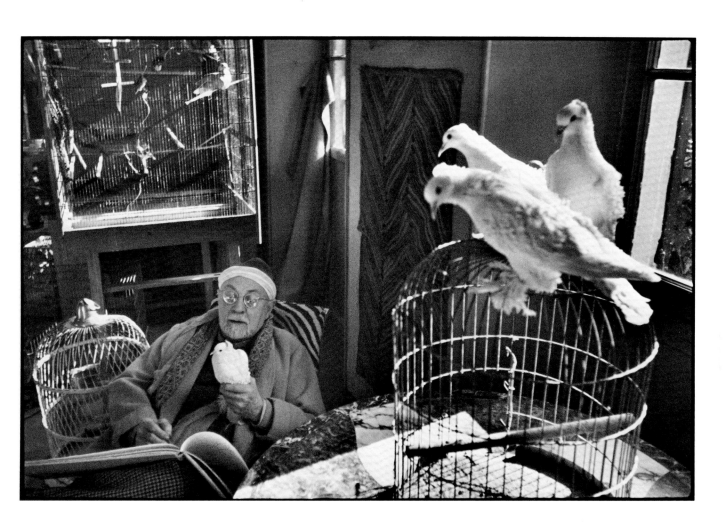

Pierre Bonnard, Le Cannet, 1944

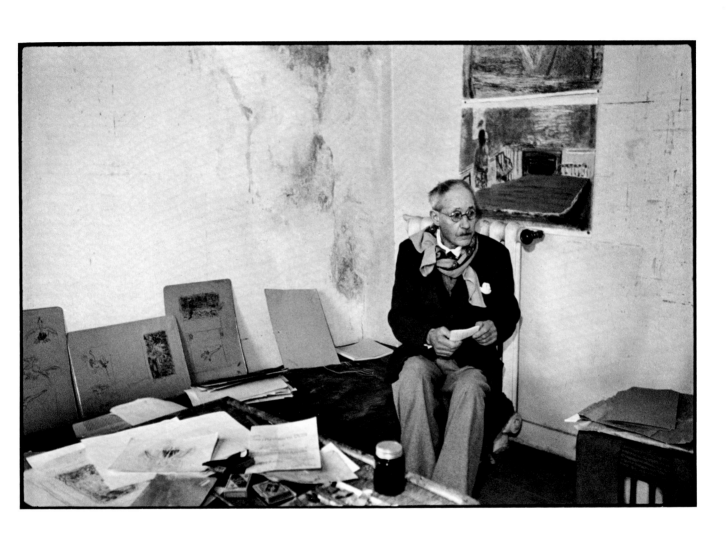

Cafeteria of the workers' building, the Hotel Metropol, Moscow, 1954

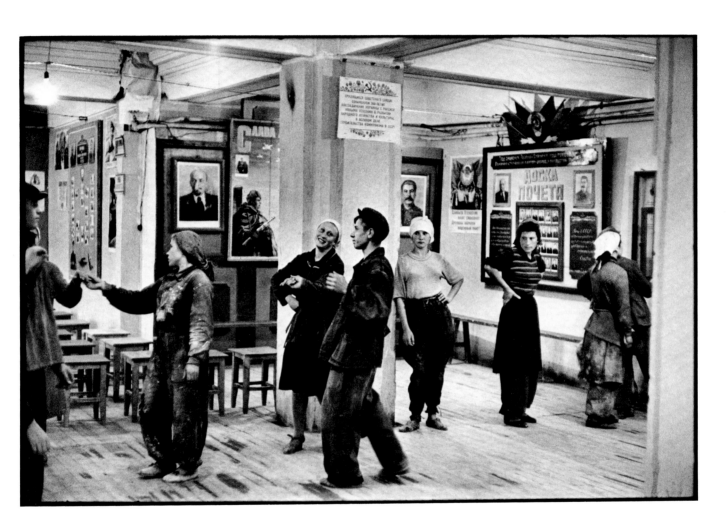

The last days of the Kuomintang, Peking, 1949

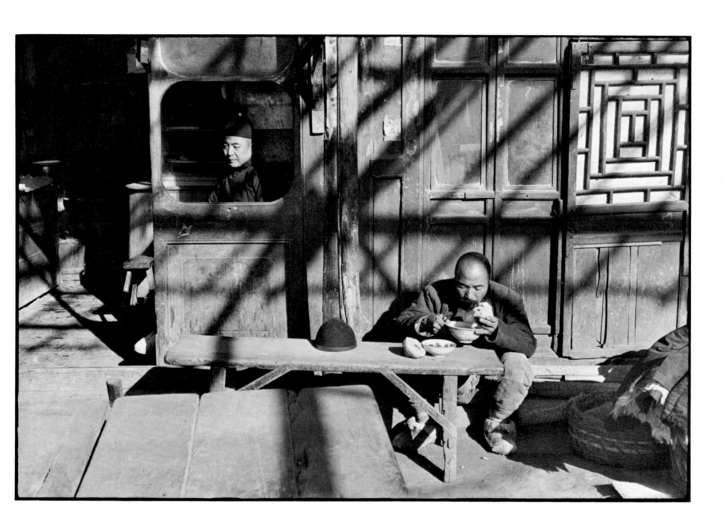

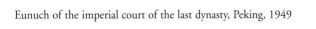
Eunuch of the imperial court of the last dynasty, Peking, 1949

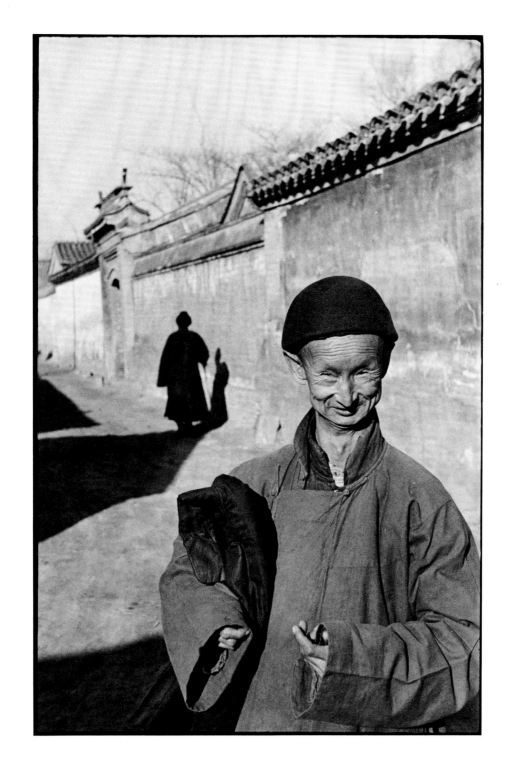

Srinagar, Kashmir, 1948

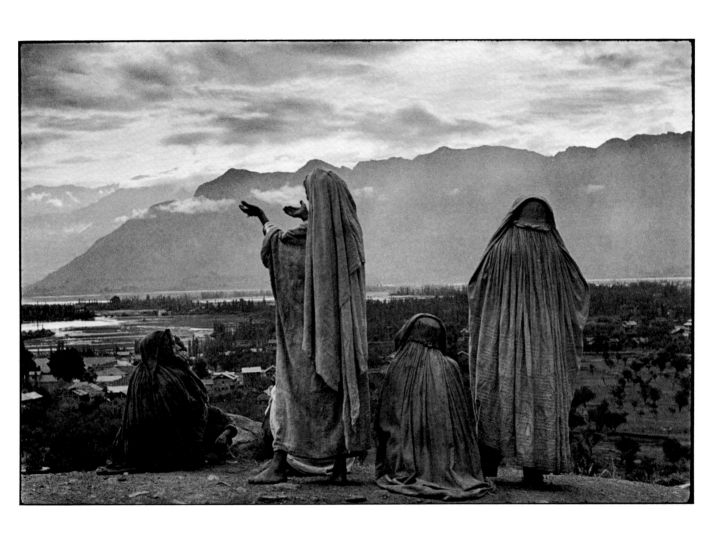

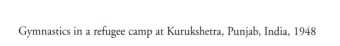

Gymnastics in a refugee camp at Kurukshetra, Punjab, India, 1948

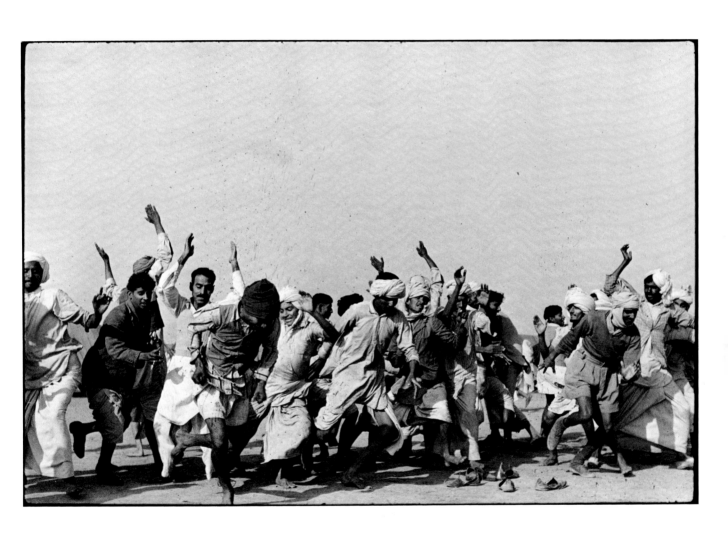

Ahmedabad, India, 1965

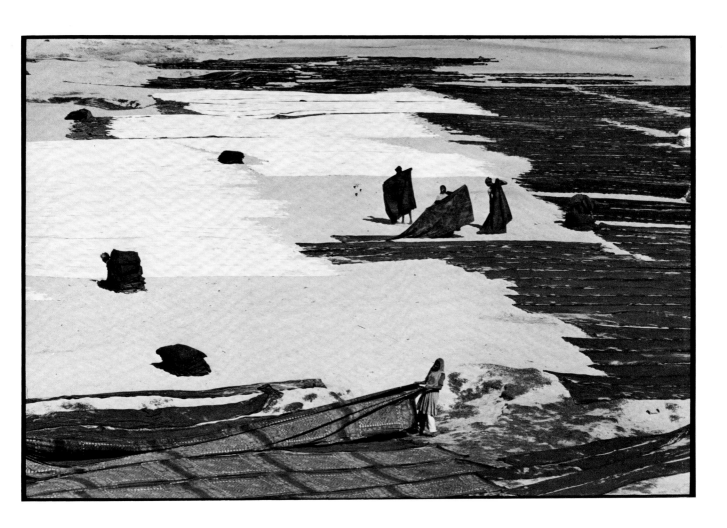

William Faulkner, Oxford, Mississippi, 1947

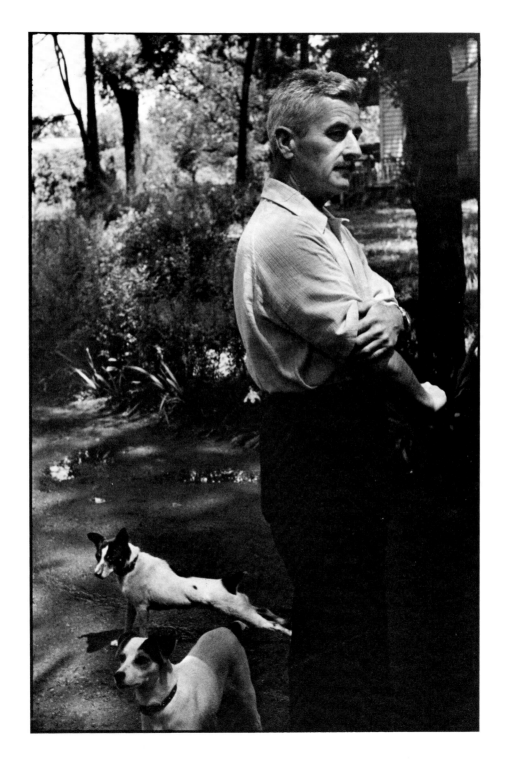

Volcano of Popocatepetl, Mexico, 1964

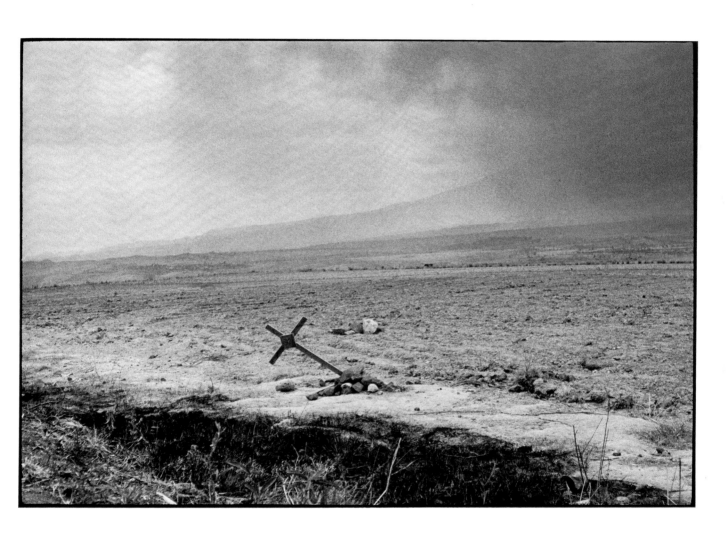

Midnight Mass at Scanno in the Abruzzi, Italy, 1953

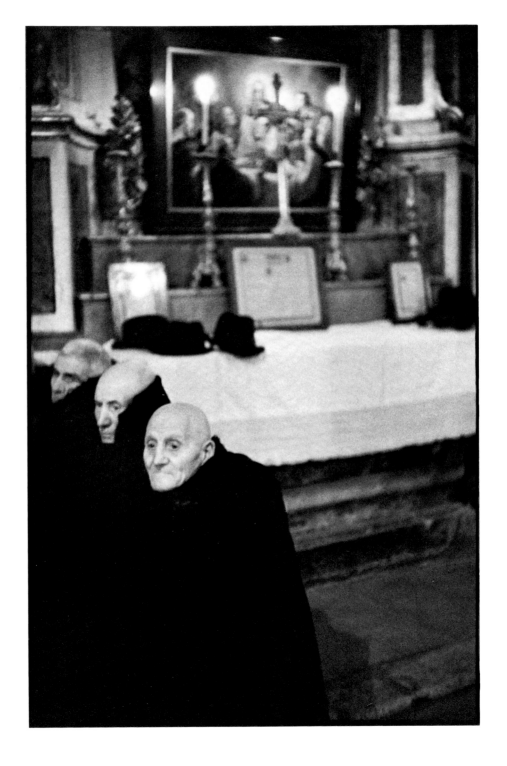

Funeral of a Kabuki actor, Japan, 1965

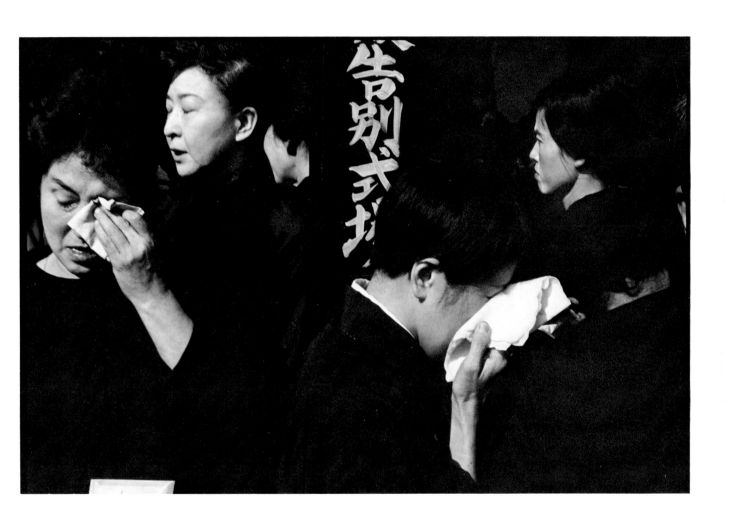

Cell in a model prison in the U.S.A., 1975

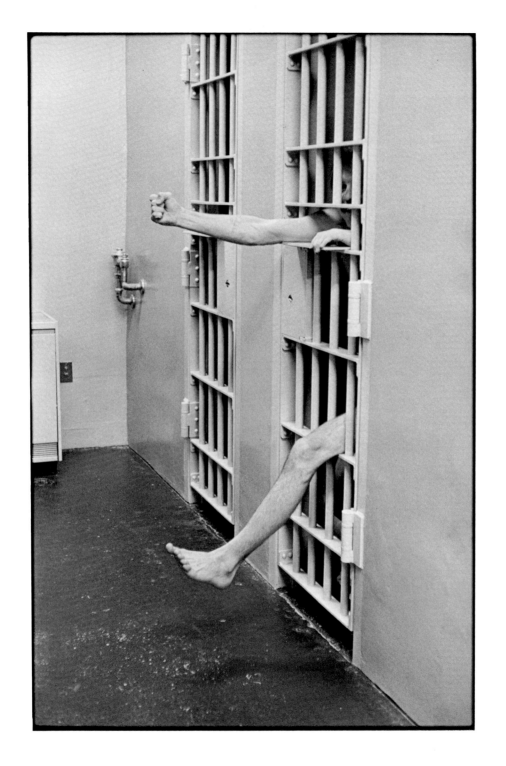

Rumania, 1975

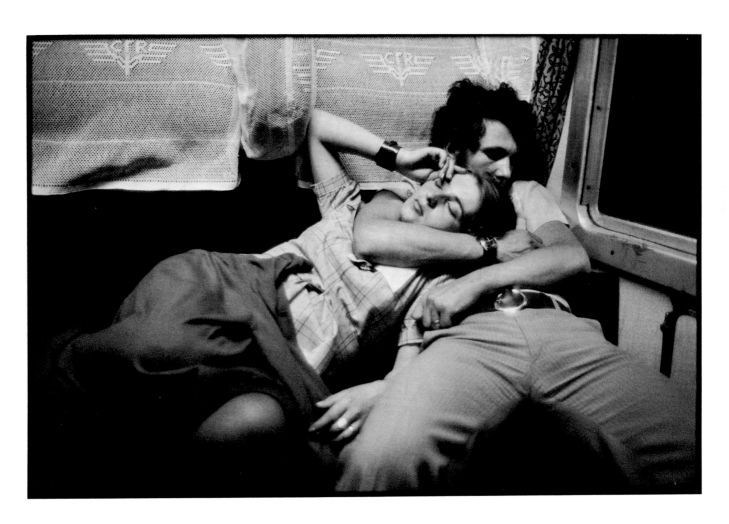

Simiane la Rotonde, 1970

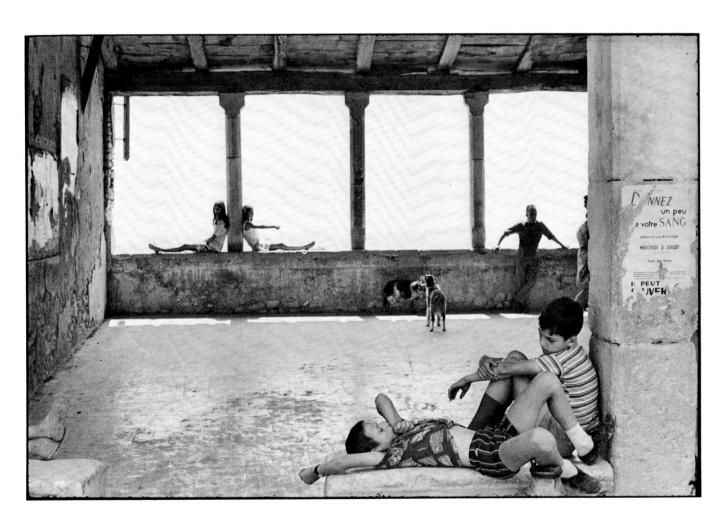

In Brie, France, June 1968

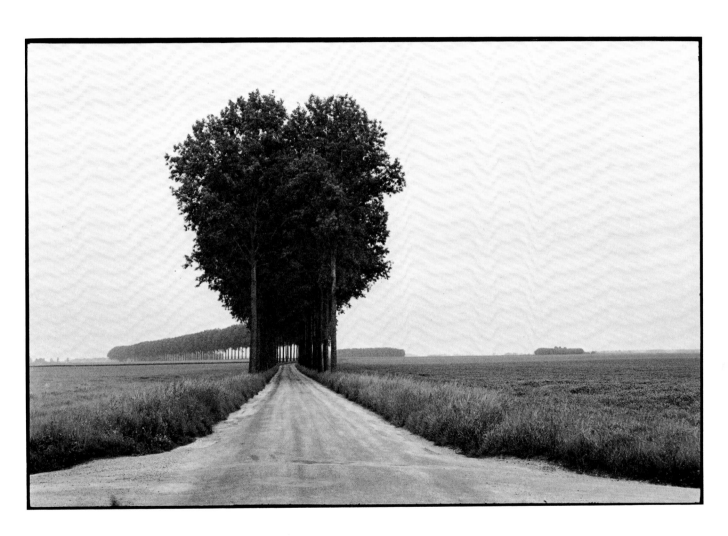

"Form is the base brought to the surface."
—VICTOR HUGO

BRIEF CHRONOLOGY

1908. Henri Cartier-Bresson is born on August 22 at Chanteloup, Seine & Marne.

1922–23. Attends the école Fénelon and the lycée Condorcet; no diplomas; develops a passionate interest in painting, and once a week studies with Cottenet.

1927–28. Studies painting with André Lhote.

1931. Spends a year on the Ivory Coast; takes up photography upon returning to Europe.

1932. His first works are exhibited at the Gallery Julien Levy, New York; then presented by Ignacio Sanchez Mejias and Guillermo de Torre at the Club Atheneo in Madrid, his first reportage is published by André in *Vu.*

1934. As photographer joins an ethnographic expedition to Mexico.

1935. Resides in the United States; studies motion pictures with Paul Strand.

1936 and 1939. Assists director Jean Renoir, with Jacques Becker and André Zvoboda.

1937. Films a documentary on hospitals in Republican Spain—*Victoire de la vie.*

1940. Is taken prisoner by the Germans; manages to escape after two vain attempts.

1943. Is active in the MNPGD, a clandestine movement to help prisoners and escapees; does portraits of artists, painters and writers (Matisse, Bonnard, Braque, Claudel, among others) for the publisher Braun.

1944–45. Joins a group of professionals who photograph the occupation of France and the liberation of Paris; shoots *Le retour,* a documentary on the homecoming of prisoners of war and the deported.

1946. Returns to the United States to complete a "posthumous" exhibition which the Museum of Modern Art in New York began in the mistaken belief that he had disappeared in the war.

1947. Founds the cooperative agency Magnum with André Capa (Bob), (Chim) David Seymour and George Rodger.

1948–50. Spends three years in the Orient, particularly in India, Burma, Pakistan, China (during the last six months of the Kuomintang and the first six of the People's Republic) and Indonesia (at the moment of its independence).

1952–53. Works in Europe.

1954. Becomes the first photographer to be admitted to the Soviet Union after restoration of international relations.

1958–59. Returns to China for three months on the occasion of the tenth anniversary of the People's Republic.

1960. Undertakes reportage in Cuba; returns to Mexico for four months; travels to Canada.

1965. Lives for six months in India and three in Japan.

1966. Leaves Magnum, but agrees to let the agency distribute his photographs to the press.

1969. Spends a year preparing an exhibition to be held at the Grand Palais in 1970—"En France"; films two documentaries for CBS News.

Since 1973. Concentrates on drawing, but takes photographs occasionally.

Honors conferred upon Henri Cartier-Bresson:

Four Overseas Press Club awards: in 1948, for his reportage on the death of Gandhi; in 1954, 1960 and 1964, for the best reportage of the year, respectively on Russia, China and Cuba.

Honorary degree of Doctor of Letters, Oxford, 1975.

Prix de la Société française de Photographie.

Prix de la Culture de la Société allemande de Photographie.

SELECTED BIBLIOGRAPHY

1947. The Photographs of Henri Cartier-Bresson. A monograph published by the Museum of Modern Art of New York. Introduction by Lincoln Kirstein and Beaumont Newhall.

1952. Images à la sauvette. Text and photos by Henri Cartier-Bresson. Cover by Matisse. Work conceived and executed by Tériade. Éditions Verve, Paris. American edition: *The Decisive Moment.* Simon & Schuster, New York.

1954. Les danses à Bali. Text on the Balinese theater by Antonin Artaud and commentary by Beryl de Zoete. Delpire Éditeur, Paris. German edition: *Bali, Tanz und Theater.* Roven Verlag Olten, 1960.

D'une Chine à l'autre. Preface by Jean-Paul Sartre. Delpire Éditeur, Paris. German edition: *China gestern und heute.* 1955. American edition: *From One China to Another.* Text by Han Suyin. Universe Books, New York, 1956. English edition: *China in Transition.* Text by Han Suyin. Thames & Hudson, London, 1956.

1955. Les Européens. Photos and introduction by Henri Cartier-Bresson. Cover by Joan Miró. Work conceived and executed by Tériade. Éditions Verve, Paris. American edition: *The Europeans.* Simon & Schuster, New York.

Moscou, vu par Henri Cartier-Bresson. Delpire Éditeur, Paris. German edition: *Menschen in Moskau.* Karl Rauch Verlag GmbH, Düsseldorf. American edition: *People of Moscow.* Simon & Schuster, New York. English edition: *People of Moscow.* Thames & Hudson, London. Italian edition: *Mosca.* Artimport, Milan.

1958. Henri Cartier-Bresson: Fotografie. Text by Anna Farova. Photos by Henri Cartier-Bresson, layout by Ropert Delpire. Statni nakladatelstvi krasne literatury hudby a umenu, narodni podnik, Prague. A Slovak edition was published in Bratislava in 1959.

1963. Photographies de Henri Cartier-Bresson. Delpire Éditeur, Paris. American edition: *Photographs by Cartier-Bresson.* Introduction by Lincoln Kirstein and Beaumont Newhall. Grossmann, New York. English edition: Jonathan Cape, London. Japanese edition: Asahi, Tokyo. German language edition: *Cartier-Bresson Meister-Aufnahmen.* Fretz & Wasmuth Verlag A.G., Zurich, 1964.

1964. China. Photos and notes on 15 months spent in China. English edition by Barbara Brakeley-Miller. Bantam Gallery, New York.

1966. The Galveston That Was. Text by Howard Barstone. Photos by Ezra Stoller and Henri Cartier-Bresson. Macmillan, New York, and the Museum of Fine Arts, Houston.

Photographs by Cartier-Bresson. Introduction by Claude Roy and Ryoichi Kojima, Asahi Shimbum, Tokyo.

1968. L'homme et la machine. Photos by Henri Cartier-Bresson, preceded by an introduction by Étiemble. Work executed under the auspices of IBM. Éditions du Chêne, Paris. American edition: *Man and Machine.* Viking Press, New York. English edition: *Man and Machine.* Thames & Hudson, London.

Flagrants délits. Delpire Éditeur, Paris. American edition: *The World of Henri Cartier-Bresson.* Viking Press, New York. German language edition: *Meine Welt, von Henri Cartier-Bresson.* Verlag Bücher, Lucerne and Frankfurt.

Impressions de Turquie. Booklet made for the Turkish Tourist Office, with an introduction by Alain Robbe-Grillet.

1970. Vive la France. Text by François Nourissier. Photos by Henri Cartier-Bresson. Published by Selection du Reader's Digest, Robert Laffont, Paris. American edition: *Cartier-Bresson's France.* Viking Press, New York. English edition: *Cartier-Bresson's France.* Thames & Hudson, London. German language edition: *Frankreich.* Verlag Bücher, Lucerne and Frankfurt.

1972. The Face of Asia. Introduction by Robert Shaplen. Published jointly by John Weatherhill (New York and Tokyo) and Orientations Ltd. (Hong Kong). French edition: *Visage d'Asie*. Éditions du Chêne, Paris.

1973. A propos de l'U.R.S.S. Éditions du Chêne, Paris. American edition: *About Russia.* Viking Press, New York. English edition: *About Russia.* Thames & Hudson, London, German language edition: *Sowjetunion, photographische Notizen von Henri Cartier-Bresson.* Verlag Bücher, Lucerne and Frankfurt.

The Decisive Moment: Henri Cartier-Bresson. Audio-visual teaching material (set of photos and interview) published in the collection *Images of Man.* Scholastic Magazines, New York.

1976. Coup d'oeil Américain. Text by Lincoln Kirstein. Special issue of *Camera*, Lucerne.

Articles (selected from numerous others) on Henri Cartier-Bresson

Beaumont Newhall, "The instant vision of Henri Cartier-Bresson." *Camera* (October, 1955)

Yvonne Baby, "'Le dur plaisir' de Henri Cartier-Bresson." *L'Express* (June, 1961).

Bob Schwalberg, "Henri Cartier-Bresson Today." *Popular Photography* (May, 1967).

Ernst Haas, "Henri Cartier-Bresson: A Lyrical View of Life." *Modern Photography* (November, 1971).

Lincoln Kirstein, "Metaphores of motion." *The Nation* (March, 1971).

Claude Roy, "Ce cher Henri." *Photo* (November, 1974).

Hilton Kramer, *The New York Times* (July 7, 1968; February 7, 1971; and March 1, 1975)

Cecil Beaton, "Henri Cartier-Bresson" *The Magic Image* (Little Brown and Co, Boston, 1975)

MAJOR EXHIBITIONS

Photographs

1932. The Gallery Julien Levy, New York (first exhibition); The Cercle Atheneo, Madrid.

1934. With Manuel Alvarez Bravo: The Palacio de Bellas Artes, Mexico.

1935. With Walker Evans: The Gallery Julien Levy, New York.

1947. The Museum of Modern Art, New York ("posthumous" exhibition).

1948. Bombay.

1952. The Institute of Contemporary Arts, London.

1953. Florence.

1955. The Musée des Arts Décoratifs, Paris (first large exhibition: 400 photos). (This exhibition traveled to various museums in Europe, then, under the auspices of the American Federation of Art, to the United States and Canada; in Japan, it was presented by Mainichi.)

1964. The Phillips Collection, Washington.

1965. Tokyo (second retrospective show, presented by Asahi). (This exhibition then went to the Musée des Arts Décoratifs, Paris, 1966–67, under the patronage of André Malraux and with the collaboration of Robert Delpire; to the Museum of Modern Art, New York, 1968; to the Victoria and Albert Museum, London, 1969; to the Stedelijk Museum, Amsterdam; to Rome, where it was organized by Balthus; to Zurich, Leverkusen, Hamburg, Bremen, Munich, Milan, Cologne, Aspen.)

1970. "En France": the Grand Palais, Paris. (This exhibition of 150 photos traveled throughout France till 1976. It has also been shown in the United States, at the Gallery Hallmark, New York, 1970; in the Soviet Union, at the Manège Museum, Moscow, 1972; in Yugoslavia, at the Museum of Modern Art, Belgrade, 1973; in Australia and in Japan, 1974.)

1974. The International Center of Photography, New York (exhibition on Russia: 1953–1974).

1975. The first international Triennial of photography presented by Michel Terrapon Fribourg, Switzerland.

Drawings

1975. The Carlton Gallery, New York (first exhibition).

1975–76. The Gallery Bischofberger, Zurich.

1976. (Summer) The Gallery Lucien Henri, Forcalquier, Alpes de Haute-Provence.

FILMS

Assistant to Jean Renoir in 1936 for *La vie est à nous* and *Une partie de campagne,* and in 1939 for *La règle du jeu.* Henri Cartier-Bresson is sole author of:

1937. Victoire de la vie. Documentary on hospitals in Republican Spain, with Jacques Lemare as cameraman. Music from Charles Koechlin.

1944–45. Le retour. Documentary on the homecoming of prisoners of war and deportees. Produced by the OWI and the Ministry of Prisoners, directed by Henri Cartier-Bresson, Lt. Banks and Capt. Krimsky, and produced by Norman Ratner.

1969–70. Two documentaries for CBS News: **Impressions of California,** with Jean Boffety as cameraman, **Southern Exposures,** with Walter Dombrow as cameraman.

Films made from stills by Henri Cartier-Bresson

1963–64. Five 15-minute films on Germany for the Süddeutscher Rundfunk, Munich.

1963. Midlands at Play and at Work. For ABC Television, London.

1964. Quebec. For the Canadian Film Board.

1967. Flagrants délits. On Henri Cartier-Bresson's work. By Robert Delpire. A Delpire production, Paris.

1970. Images de France. By Liliane de Kermadec for O.R.T.F. An Unité Trois production.

1975. Why New Jersey. For WNET, New York.

Salerno, Italy, 1933

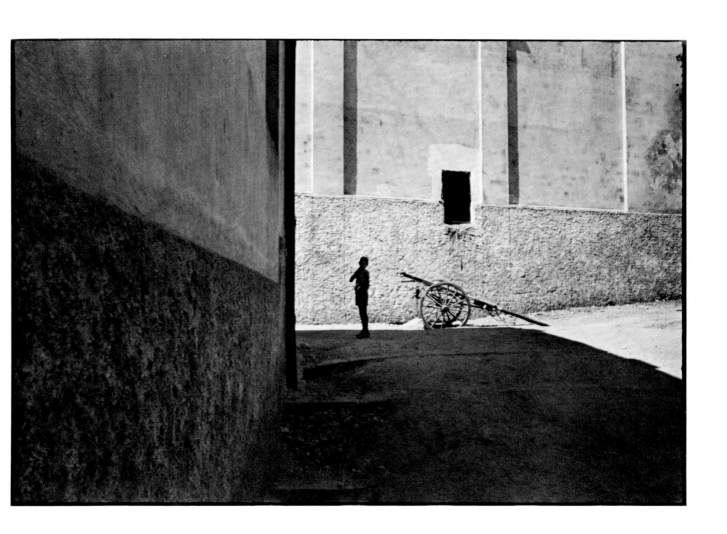

APERTURE Masters of Photography

The Aperture Masters of Photography series provides a comprehensive library of photographers who have shaped the medium in important ways.

Each volume presents a selection of the photographer's greatest images. 96 pages, 8 x 8 inches, 42 black-and-white photographs; hardcover, $12.50. The set of twelve titles, a $150 value, is available for $99.95 and can be purchased through fine bookstores.

If unavailable from your bookseller, contact Aperture, 20 East 23rd Street, New York, NY 10010. Toll Free: (800) 929-2323; Tel: (212) 598-4205; Fax: (212) 598-4015.

A complete catalog of Aperture books is available on request.

BERENICE ABBOTT
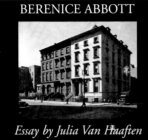
Essay by Julia Van Haaften

EUGENE ATGET
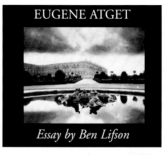
Essay by Ben Lifson

MANUEL ALVAREZ BRAVO
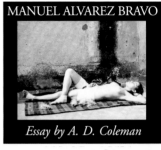
Essay by A. D. Coleman

HENRI CARTIER-BRESSON
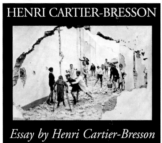
Essay by Henri Cartier-Bresson

WALKER EVANS
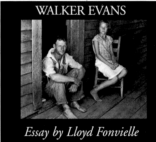
Essay by Lloyd Fonvielle

ANDRE KERTESZ
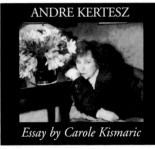
Essay by Carole Kismaric

MAN RAY
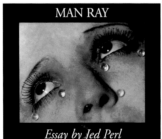
Essay by Jed Perl

AUGUST SANDER
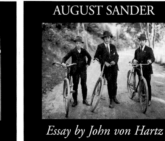
Essay by John von Hartz

ALFRED STIEGLITZ
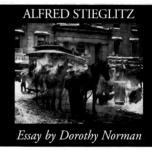
Essay by Dorothy Norman

PAUL STRAND
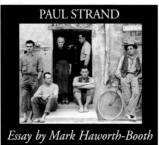
Essay by Mark Haworth-Booth

WEEGEE
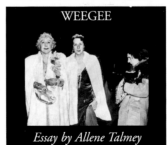
Essay by Allene Talmey

EDWARD WESTON
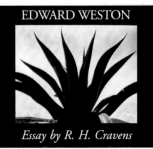
Essay by R. H. Cravens